# For You When I Am Gone

_____

**A JOURNAL**

_____

# For You When I Am Gone

---

## A JOURNAL

---

### A Step-by-Step Guide
### to Writing Your Ethical Will

Steve Leder

Avery

an imprint of Penguin Random House
New York

Library of Congress Control Number: 2022937471

Trade paperback ISBN: 9780593421574
Ebook ISBN: 9780593543245

Printed in the United States of America
1st Printing

Book design by Shannon Nicole Plunkett

# Contents

# Introduction

"How do you do it?" people often ask me. "How do you sit with family after family when their loved one has died to listen to their stories, to hold their pain, and to help them smile and laugh in the midst of that pain? Doesn't it exhaust you? After thirty-five years and more than a thousand funerals, aren't you tired of it all?" My answer is sincere and always the same. "Exhausted? Yes. Tired of it? Never." Why not? Because every person's life is amazing. Everyone has a powerful, beautiful, bittersweet story. But that story reveals itself only if you ask the right questions in the right order. Revealing the uniqueness and essence of a person's life is an art.

This guided journal will help you tell your own story. It asks the questions I have posed and refined over more than three decades to enable your life, your love, your values, your vulnerability, and your dreams to unfold for your loved ones when you are gone like a flower blossoming in time-lapse photography—extraordinary, exquisite, and astonishing.

People have been writing ethical wills or legacy letters for a very long time to let those they will leave behind benefit from their hard-earned wisdom and their love. The earliest that remains dates back almost a thousand years. And yet, despite ten centuries of examples of people who have written and bequeathed their life lessons, values, and love to their children, grandchildren, other family, and friends, most people don't. Some of us have an estate plan for which we carefully decided how much money, if any, and what "stuff" our loved ones will inherit when we die. All of that is important. But I have learned over the years that money and material objects are not what your loved ones will want or need the most to help comfort and inspire them when you are no longer there. They want *you*— your guidance when they are lost, your wisdom when they are conflicted, your laughter and your empathy when they are sad, your forgiveness when they stumble. These matters of the heart are the most precious legacy of your life and no estate plan can ever bestow them upon the people you love. But you can.

We are not all expert writers, but we are experts when it comes to knowing about our own lives. And with some guidance, every one of us can turn that knowledge into a priceless legacy. Ask me to build a coffee table and the coffee table will never materialize. But hand me the pieces and clear directions, and—with a little effort, cursing, a missing part here or there, and a sense of great pride once completed—the coffee table will take shape. With questions, explanations, and pithy, hopefully inspiring bits I selected from hundreds of sermons I have written over the years, this book will guide you to identify and assemble the important pieces of your story. It will hold your hand the entire way, just as I would the loved ones of someone who is gone and did not take the time to write down what they most wanted those they cared about to know. Don't let that someone be you someday.

If you came to this book because you read my last one, *For You When I Am Gone: Twelve Essential Questions to Tell a Life Story*, great. You already know about ethical wills and why these questions matter and you've gotten a taste of other people's answers. But perhaps you didn't find time to put the book down and answer the questions for yourself. I hope the space to write in this book will inspire you to do that now. For those who have not read my last book, this one is meant to stand alone, giving you what you need to create an ethical will of your own.

You will be amazed at what pours out of your heart and soul as you wrestle with the questions in these pages. Your honest answers will tell a truth about who and what really matters in your life that your loved ones will cherish for the rest of theirs when you are gone. Let's begin. . . .

CHAPTER 1

# What Do You Regret?

We all regret things we have said and done. But most people's greatest regrets are not the things they have said or done, but the things they failed to do or say. We can enlighten our loved ones far greater by sharing our deepest regrets than by touting our tales of chances taken or battles won. Satisfaction teaches us little, but there is an instructive sting to opportunities missed: the could haves and should haves of our lives. The times we knowingly turned away from love and meaning, challenge and duty, beauty and joy, are hard to forget. If we cannot forget our regrets, if we cannot undo the past, then let us include them in the legacy we leave for the ones we love. Regret requires introspection and honesty; it is a great and wise teacher when we are brave enough to face it. There is no way to create a meaningful life or a meaningful legacy lesson without that courage.

What is your biggest regret and how can your loved ones avoid the same? What do you wish you had done, why, and what will doing those things hopefully bring to your loved ones' lives that you missed out on?

_____

_____

_____

_____

_____

_____

_____

_____

_____

_____

_____

_____

_____

_____

_____

_____

_____

*It's simple, really—with friends to tell us when we are wrong, we arrive together at the truth. Without them, truth dies.*

---

*The sins of long ago are mostly no different from the sins of today: a little gossip, some arrogance, a half-truth, fraud, anger, narrow-mindedness. In one sense nothing much has changed in twenty centuries.*

---

---

*You would think a rabbi would be secure enough in himself to know that appearances matter little and character, ability, dedication, and passion count for much. But for more than three decades, I have worried about looking the part of the rabbi for you. That meant a closet filled with twenty suits, forty shirts, dozens of ties and shoes and belts from Italy and Paris. I don't know how many hours and how many tens of thousands of dollars or more I have spent over thirty-four years, dressing the part of rabbi. I am going to stay looser when this whole pandemic is over. Less phony, more comfortable, more trusting that each of you knows and sees the real me no matter what I am wearing.*

---

We all make a choice about what we remember.
Do we self-righteously remember the wrongs done to us
or humbly recall the wrongs we committed ourselves?

_____

_____

_____

_____

_____

_____

_____

_____

_____

_____

_____

_____

_____

_____

_____

_____

_____

_____

―――――――――――――――――――――――

*Only doubt and humility will heal us. Only doubt and humility make forgiveness possible. Without them, we are lost.*

―――――――――――――――――――――――

*There is a wholeness about the person who has learned that they can live through their own mistakes, who can lose someone through divorce or estrangement or foolishness and still feel like a complete person. Missing something makes us human, humane, and whole.*

In ancient times repentance and forgiveness were easy. The high priest laid both hands on a goat, confessed over it all the iniquities of his people, and set it free. Next, an animal was sacrificed. Amidst the smell of burning flesh mingled with incense, the people returned from their temple magically purified and renewed. But we are modern people, removed from magic and superstition. What are we supposed to do? The answer, I would suggest, is in the question:

*What would I do if I had it to do all over again?*

_____

_____

_____

_____

_____

_____

_____

_____

_____

_____

_____

_____

How can we plead for mercy, compassion, and forgiveness for ourselves but not be compassionate, merciful, and forgiving of others?

_____

_____

_____

_____

_____

_____

_____

_____

_____

_____

_____

_____

_____

_____

_____

_____

_____

_____

My high school friend Neal's grandfather had a simple way
of summing up forgiveness that I will always remember.
He put it this way: "What was was, what is is, and that's
that." Will our future be different from our past?
Will we forgive and open our arms and hearts wide
so that love does not die—and that's that?

_____

_____

_____

_____

_____

_____

_____

_____

_____

_____

_____

_____

_____

_____

_____

_____

# CHAPTER 2

# When Was a Time You Led with Your Heart?

I cannot think of anything worse than being called heartless. To be heartless is to be capable of cruelty without conscience, or to be little more than a living, breathing algorithm, a human calculator of odds. To lead with our hearts, by contrast, is to be true to our deepest selves and what we hold most dear. Leading with our hearts is not the same as reckless abandon. It is a feeling more than a thought, faith more than a considered judgment, a commitment to the truth—sometimes, in spite of the facts. Of course, there are times in our lives—most in fact—when it is right to consider risk and reward before acting. Most of the time we should "use our heads." And yet our lives are most profoundly and beautifully shaped by those rare, liberating moments when we think, and then act, from the heart. Your example will inspire your loved ones to lead with their own hearts when it matters most, and that will likely lead to the greatest decisions of their lives.

When was a time you led with your heart rather than with
your head? Why and how did that change your life?

_____

_____

_____

_____

_____

_____

_____

_____

_____

_____

_____

_____

_____

_____

_____

_____

_____

_____

What if this is the day we really are strong and courageous? Strong and courageous enough to live in harmony with our most secret hopes and dreams? Strong and courageous enough to turn toward the vision, the hope, and the rapture of our most precious dreams?

_____

_____

_____

_____

_____

_____

_____

_____

_____

_____

_____

_____

_____

_____

_____

I call the couch in my office the "Couch of Tears." People often sit there to pour out their sorrows, to weep, to ask, "Why?" When it is their marriage that is the source of those tears, the answer to why is often very simple. Somewhere on the journey that was their marriage, they just stopped being nice to each other. They stopped being kind to each other. Do you want to stay married? Be kind. Do you want to hold on to your kids even when they are adults themselves? Be kind. Do you want to be close to your brothers and sisters, your elderly parents? Do you want to have friends? Do you want to be respected and successful in business? Do you want to be proud of who you are—who you really are? Be kind. Think with your heart.

_____

_____

_____

_____

_____

_____

_____

_____

_____

To whom are you grateful? Do they know?
Have you told him? Have you told her?

_____

_____

_____

_____

_____

_____

_____

_____

_____

_____

_____

_____

_____

_____

_____

_____

_____

_____

---

*A few months ago, I asked the soon-to-be graduates of our elementary school what the single most important thing was that they had learned over the past seven years. Not one of them, not one, said that the most important thing they learned was math, science, history, grammar, vocabulary, geography, or technology. Each of them in their own way said virtually the same thing—the most important thing they had learned in school was kindness, to be a welcoming, thoughtful, considerate, caring, kind person.*

---

*What I said to those precious children in that classroom about to enter middle school was, "No matter how many facts you have learned here, if you are not prepared to hold fast to the most important truth you have learned here—you cannot go out into the world. You cannot go out into the world unless you are committed to being a kind person. You cannot leave here unless you are committed to changing the world and not allowing the world to change you. You cannot leave here unless you keep your promise to be the only thing that matters—a kind, caring, humane human being. That is your and that is our world's only hope."*

_Thanking strangers for a job well done is easy compared to telling the people closest to us that they matter, that we are grateful to them and proud of them._

*We all walk past the rubble of other people's lives now and then. When the life of someone we know falls to pieces, it's our job to be "compassionate and gracious, slow to anger, abounding in kindness" (Psalm 103:8), reaching out to gather up the people we love, granting them dignity and holding them in the holiest of places, our hearts.*

*My friend's son died by suicide. This friend was the cool, hip rabbi at the summer camp I went to as a kid. I became a rabbi in part because I wanted to be like him. Here's a part of the eulogy he gave to honor his son: "We are brokenhearted. We cannot hide our brokenness. Let me tell you what we know: Each of you would willingly give us a piece of your heart if it would help to make ours whole. We know, we know. For us, that is the only intimation that the laws of gravity might one day be restored." A piece of our hearts, willingly given, the heart of another gratefully received. The ebb and flow of friendship and love, care and kindness, kindness—is the only thing that enables any of us to go on.*

CHAPTER 3

# What Makes You Happy?

Many cultures have a folktale about searching for buried treasure. Usually, the protagonist sets off on a long journey, seeking the riches that will lead to happiness. The search takes many years over many miles, perilous roads, and hidden danger. Eventually each seeker returns home empty-handed and seemingly defeated, only to discover treasure buried right there all along. It is easy to be seduced into believing some things will make us happy, only to find out that what really brings us happiness is a meaningful life spent loving and being loved, come what may. It takes a long time for most of us to realize what truly matters and what it means to be happy, and these discoveries are worth sharing. Things can be expensive but not precious; things can make us feel good, but that is not the same thing as happiness. What and who make you happy? Why? Your loved ones will want to know when your journey ends. . . .

What makes you happy, and what lesson is there
in the things that make you happy that you
can share with your loved ones?

_____

_____

_____

_____

_____

_____

_____

_____

_____

_____

_____

_____

_____

_____

_____

_____

_____

*It doesn't take much, especially now, for us to dwell on the dark side of life. On the other hand, thinking about the best, most beautiful parts of life takes work. Awe, joy, gratitude, happiness even, are the result of a deliberate, disciplined, daily commitment—a forcing of oneself to seek and embrace something hopeful and good, no matter how small.*

*Since my back surgery, instead of hiking and climbing with my old aggression, I now walk slowly into the desert and sit on a boulder. In that sitting I see the desert I had never seen or felt before. And I pray in a way I have never prayed before. The prayer comes to me. God comes to me. To be in nature is to feel a part of something larger and more beautiful than our suffering.*

Try this experiment recommended for depression by psychologist Martin Seligman. He calls it a "Gratitude Visit." Seligman asks his subjects to close their eyes and remember someone who did something enormously important that changed their lives in a good way and whom they never properly thanked. The person has to be alive. I hope all of us have such a person. Now, the assignment is to write a three-hundred-word testimonial to that person. Call them on the phone and ask if you can visit; don't tell them why. Show up at the door, then read your testimonial—everyone weeps when this happens. When Seligman tests both the visitor and the person visited one week later, a month later, three months later, they are both happier and less depressed.

_____

_____

_____

_____

_____

_____

_____

_____

_____

_____

_Consider the Chinese proverb: "If you want happiness
for an hour—take a nap. If you want happiness for a day—go
fishing. If you want happiness for a month—get married.
If you want happiness for a year—inherit a fortune.
If you want happiness for a lifetime—help others." It's true.
We are at our best, our happiest; we are closest to God,
when we are helping another person._

---

*Imagine what our country would be like if the
American ideal was life, liberty, and the pursuit of goodness.
Imagine a nation filled with people pursuing goodness
rather than their own happiness.*

---

*We tend to think of joy as a singular, spontaneous moment in time caused by external factors we do not control—a sort of lucky surprise like winning the lottery without buying a ticket. But the religious understanding of joy views it as part of a process, the distillate of mindful living day after week after month and even after decades of intention.*

---

*I was sad on my way home. I turned the radio off in
the car because I needed quiet. I needed to be alone. I needed
to think. I'm not used to burying people my own age. It cuts
close to home. It hurts. During that sad ride home from the
cemetery, numb on the freeway, one heavy truth, one cruel
cliché weighs upon me. "Life is short," I keep repeating.
"Life is short." Slowly, the melancholy lifts. There are a few
errands to run and my kids make me laugh at dinner.
By that evening I feel alive again.*

---

What is it for you? Amidst the terrible news and uncertainty, what light, what joy, what tiny, precious moment from this past week did you cherish? What quiet miracle did you embrace? Tonight, tell the people you love about it. Tonight, choose life. Because life . . . is beautiful.

_____

_____

_____

_____

_____

_____

_____

_____

_____

_____

_____

_____

_____

_____

_____

_____

*Not only do we have no idea what will ultimately make us happy, but we also have no idea just how happy we already are.*

# CHAPTER 4

# What Was Your Biggest Failure?

While we likely wish it were otherwise, the truth is that we learn more from failure than success. Success encourages us to keep doing the same things over and over again. Failure is disruptive. Failure is life changing. When we stumble out of arrogance or haste, hesitation or harshness, carelessness or foolishness, the result can be serrated and sharp, scarring us in ways impossible to deny. But why deny our greatest failures? Denial is the only thing that makes failure permanent. To remember our failures not only as failures, but as lessons learned, chances taken, disruption along the road of repetition, detours that led to new ways, is to make those failures our greatest successes. Like regret, failure too is a great and wise teacher. Let your failures guide your loved ones now and when you are gone.

What was your biggest failure and what lesson did you learn
that is worth sharing with your loved ones?

_____

_____

_____

_____

_____

_____

_____

_____

_____

_____

_____

_____

_____

_____

_____

_____

_____

_____

_____

*We all feel locked in sometimes—trapped in yesterday's ways, misunderstood, distant from our dreams. But our stories are not yet fully written in the book of life.*

*For the times we could have said "I love you" and failed,*
*forgive us, pardon us, grant us atonement.*

---

*If you grew up the way I did, inaction was the paradigmatic sin.
But deep down, I know better. I know I must admit my
emptiness and fatigue, embrace and make peace with them.
Tonight and tomorrow, I will surrender.*

---

---

*Perhaps this can be the year we reach out for help,
stop hiding so well, and get found.*

---

It is time to be honest with ourselves. What have we accomplished? Where did we fail? Did we love and give care and hope, or did we smother with petty jealousy and anger? Did we pretend to care about things bright and holy while secretly holding them in contempt? Did we lie? Did we turn away from the suffering in the world or did we reach out to make a difference? What did we do behind closed doors, in the bedroom, in the boardroom? What did we say to wound a loved one's heart?

_____

_____

_____

_____

_____

_____

_____

_____

_____

_____

_____

_____

_____

*"I'm sorry. Please forgive me. Apology accepted" are some of the most difficult words in the entire English language.*

How many times has each of us failed to walk those twenty feet to our unfinished business? Twenty feet away from the stack of unread books. Twenty feet away from the exercise bike. Twenty feet from the telephone. From our brother or sister, our kids, our marriages, and our friendships evaporating from neglect. Twenty feet away from all the unfinished business in our lives and we do nothing. Oh, I know that some unfinished business can never be resolved; there's no sin in that. It's not trying that's a tragic shame.

_____

_____

_____

_____

_____

_____

_____

_____

_____

_____

_____

_____

# CHAPTER 5

# What Got You Through Your Greatest Challenge?

When someone is facing what they describe as the worst thing that has ever happened to them, I always ask the same question. "What was the second worst thing?" They always know that answer. Then I ask them how they got through the thing that until now was the worst thing that had ever happened to them. Here again, with a little thought, people almost always know. It might have been leaning on friends or family, seeking therapy, tending to their physical and spiritual well-being, or simply allowing for the passage of time. I remind them that this new challenge, much like the previous one, has not robbed them of their ability or changed their personality. They can have faith that what worked before will very likely work again, and probably even better as a result of experience. Whatever the particulars of a difficult situation, it is this faith that gets us through—faith in ourselves to survive yet again. The people you care about will need this faith. You can give it to them.

What enabled you to withstand and move on in the face of your greatest challenge? What advice can you offer your loved ones to guide them when they encounter real adversity?

_____

_____

_____

_____

_____

_____

_____

_____

_____

_____

_____

_____

_____

_____

_____

What is it? What is in you, your family, your work, your world that is broken that only you can repair? You are great enough to find it. You are great enough to repair it.

_____

_____

_____

_____

_____

_____

_____

_____

_____

_____

_____

_____

_____

_____

_____

_____

_____

_____

*Life ends, and we cannot change that. Not with love, not with strength, not with science, not with faith, not with anything. Death wins, always. And if that person you loved so deeply is mortal, then you too shall someday surely die. We really are only human. To be at peace with our helplessness—and I am not yet—is the most terrible and powerful of lessons.*

_Ten years of Alzheimer's. Ten damn years. The last five in a diaper and a bib, staring from his wheelchair into the distance, listless and lost. Why? I am a rabbi. I am supposed to understand these things. I do not. But I do know what God said to Job. And I know what my dad said when we told him about his diagnosis, and what he would have said standing next to me in the kitchen last night as the candle flickered: "Es iz vas es iz—It is what it is." Sometimes, "Why?" is the wrong question._

---

*Grief ebbs and flows, ebbs and flows, ebbs and flows.*
*Sometimes we can stand up in it. Other times it pulls us under,*
*thrashes and scares us; the world is upside down and we*
*cannot breathe. When that wave called grief comes, it is*
*best to float with the pain and the emptiness, give in to it,*
*be with it, take your time, and then stand up again.*

---

*We stand to do battle once again with our*
*secrets and our demons.*

---

*I would rather be uncomfortable than indifferent. That's the problem with being too comfortable, isn't it? Comfort requires a certain kind of blindness to the world and its brokenness. We can do so much in the world if we are willing to look and to see, to really see where it is broken. Serving God and humanity guarantees meaning and purpose in our lives; it makes us part of a community that will care for us when sorrow comes. It does not guarantee the lack of sorrow.*

---

*When you are in pain, when you are lost, when you are afraid—*
*double down on your relationships. Cherish them. Nurture*
*them. No one—no one—endures suffering better alone.*
*Do not let the centrifuge of life's sorrows and stresses whirl*
*your family and your friendships apart. Double down.*
*Make things right with the people you love. For only love*
*can lift us from our suffering and our fear.*

---

*Every one of us sooner or later walks through hell.*
*The hell of cancer, the hell of that reluctant shovelful of*
*earth upon the body of someone we deeply loved, the hell*
*of betrayal, the hell of betraying, the hell of divorce, the*
*hell of a kid in trouble, the hell of Alzheimer's, the hell of*
*addiction, the hell of hiding, the hell of aging. Everyone goes*
*through hell. The point is not to come out empty-handed.*
*The point is to find some meaning in having gone through*
*hell, to make your life worthy of your suffering.*

---

# CHAPTER 6

# What Is a Good Person?

Many times since my father's death, I have said to myself and to others, "I know exactly what Dad would say right now and exactly how he would say it." I carry the treasure of his wisdom. Even in death, he guides me. We are born morally neutral and learn from others what it means to be good. We are shaped by the way they treated us and taught us. But our moral compass, and those of our loved ones, is also directed by religion, coaches, therapists, philosophers, thought leaders, movies, literature, pop culture, social media, and more. These forces are not neutral. Some are virtuous and good, others filled with objectification and hate. Most of us strive to be good people and hope that we inspire our loved ones to do the same. But we can do more than hope. We can take the time to actually tell them what being a good person means to us, handing them our own compass to guide them for the rest of their lives.

What does it mean to be a good person?

---

*The world that God creates is called "good."*
*Not perfect. Not great. Just "good."*
*Making a good world better is up to us, not God.*

---

Will we pray to become better or simply better off?

_____

_____

_____

_____

_____

_____

_____

_____

_____

_____

_____

_____

_____

_____

_____

_____

_____

_____

_____

---

*We are all pretty good at judging others. But we have
such a hard time seeing ourselves—such a hard time seeing
the pettiness, the contempt, the stubbornness, the arrogance,
the fear, the weakness, the foolishness, the anger,
the dismissiveness, the brokenness.*

---

*There is great power, the greatest power, in humility.*

---

*Everyone should have two pockets, each containing*
*a slip of paper. On one should be written: "The world was*
*created for me." But on the other: "I am but dust and ash."*
*It is the tension between these two points of view*
*that leads to true wisdom.*

*We create worlds, we create light, we destroy worlds,
we spread darkness, with words.* Avra Kehdabra—*we create,
as we speak. We can destroy ourselves, and we can destroy
others with words. We sometimes forget that we should live
our lives assuming what we say will be heard. But if words
can destroy us and the people we love, if words can hurt,
then it must also be true that words can heal.*

---

*There is a beautiful old story about a student who came to a rabbi and said, "In the olden days there were those who saw the face of God. Why don't they anymore?" The rabbi replied, "Because nowadays no one can stoop low enough." Let us all be great enough to stoop low.*

---

---

*We can become better people by choosing how not to behave.*
*Because what we choose not to do, not to say, not to envy,*
*not to hold on to from within any longer, because of what*
*we remove from our hearts and lives, the true light of*
*who we really can be shines upon our innermost soul.*

---

_I want to live a beautiful life so that beauty is what
remains within the people I leave behind when I am gone.
We are helpless in death but we are not helpless in life._

CHAPTER 7

# What Is Love?

Love is impossible to fully define or describe with words, music, art, or even a touch. But we know when we feel it and when we don't. My wife once described love in only two words: "ice cream." That might sound silly, but the more she elaborated, the more sense it made. Ice cream is sweet and satisfying whether hard or soft, plain or full of crazy stuff, dipped in a cone, scooped in a dish, or plopped on warm pie. Ice cream makes us feel better. It's good from the beginning to the very end.

Of course, not everything about love is sweet. Love is sacrifice, real and difficult. Love is painful and petty sometimes. To love is to care about the needs of another more than our own, a sacred covenant in which we affirm that we and they are one, a gain from the loss of our autonomy, a receiving that can be found only in giving.

Words are blunt and imperfect tools, but they are the best we have. However indescribable and uncapturable, we know love and the blessings of its powerful presence. Tell your loved ones about your love for them. There are no perfect words for love, but words of love are precious still.

What is love?

_____

_____

_____

_____

_____

_____

_____

_____

_____

_____

_____

_____

_____

_____

_____

_____

If you are sitting next to someone you truly love tonight and that someone truly loves you, you are in the presence of greatness. For what is greater than love?

---

*Whoever said "Being in love means never having to say you are sorry" was an idiot. The truth is, being in love means finding new ways to say you are sorry, over and over and over and over again. The success or failure of every relationship—husbands and wives, parents and children, brothers and sisters, partners and friends—depends almost entirely on our capacity to seek and to grant forgiveness.*

---

*It is who, not what, we have that makes our lives meaningful.*

---

*No matter how many times we hold each other, kiss and love each other, and no matter how many times we say "I love you"—it is never enough. So let us write of our love to those for whom our words can bring comfort, meaning, and love long after we are gone.*

*"On three, Dad. One, two, three—up we go. That's it.
Don't let go," a man reminded his old, sick father as he slowly
lifted him off the couch so that they were now face-to-face.
The old man's body slumped against his son's, his arms locked
in place behind his son's neck; the son's arms were around his
father's waist. Then the dance began—the most tender dance I
have ever seen. "That's it, Dad," the younger man encouraged
as he slowly rocked from side to side as his father shuffled
each foot, still grasping his son with all his strength. Ever so
gently, the son inched them both toward the bedroom, where
his father could lie down and have his diaper changed.
"That's it. Good, Dad. Now I know why Mom said you were such
a great dancer." Side to side. Inch by inch. The old man and his
middle-aged son holding on to each other against the sadness
and the ache—swaying to a melody only they could hear.*

*It is the simple fact that we do not have forever that*
*makes our love for each other so profound.*

*It's the way I look at my wife after thirty-seven years and say with a deep sense of satisfaction, "We're old and married." It's how good we have become at forgiving each other. We have to be. Those of us who have managed to stay married for a decade or two or six understand that marriage is about being in the same boat far from shore, riding out the lift and settle, the lift and settle, learning to get over it, whatever it is.*

When a husband holds his wife or she holds him in the middle of a dark, dark night, not during triumph, but in his or her defeat, when broken, in paralyzing pain, and in tears; that holding—that is greatness. When a parent loves a child in his or her most disappointing and foolish moment—that is greatness. When we reach out to treat another who is suffering the way we ourselves would want to be treated, not with cruel judgment, but with mercy and compassion— that is greatness. And what is greater than love?

# CHAPTER 8

# Have You Ever Cut Someone Out of Your Life?

The first thing I learned when I trained to become a lifeguard as a teenager was "Throw, row, go." In other words, if a person is drowning, the best thing to do is throw them a flotation device so they can save themselves. The second best thing is to get to them quickly by boat. The worst option is to get in the water. The reason is that when you approach a drowning person in the water, their instinct is to push you down in order to lift themselves up enough to breathe. The strength of a desperate person can be overwhelming, and as a result, rescuers can drown while trying to save the drowning.

Life is like that too sometimes. Someone we know, love even, may be so deeply troubled, so toxic, so flawed, that no matter how many times we try to help them, no matter how many chances we give them, they end up pushing us down. Severe narcissism is real, so are physical and emotional abuse. Sometimes, addiction or mental illness is incurable; and just because you throw and row does not make it right to go. There is much to learn from piercing the denial of another's effect on you and your own limitations to rescue or change them. Share what you have learned with your loved ones so they are never pushed down so far that they become the victim.

Did you ever have to cut someone out of your life?
What lesson is there within that decision to guide
your loved ones in their relationships?

_____

_____

_____

_____

_____

_____

_____

_____

_____

_____

_____

*Is it right to carry bitterness in our hearts for someone who
has done what we ourselves have also done? Maybe it is,
if the person who hurt us shows no remorse. If that person has
not stopped, has not apologized, will never stop or apologize,
then it's true that we do not have to forgive. But we can let go,
move on, make peace with what they will never be—we
can release ourselves from their grasp.*

_Someone asked Rabbi Shlomo Carlebach, a folk singer and teacher who came to America from Vienna as a teenager because of the Nazis, why he went back to Vienna to give concerts. "Don't you hate them?" he was asked. His answer was this: "If I had two souls, I would devote one to hating them. But since I only have one, I don't want to waste it hating." A sentence so simple, so healthy, and so wise that I think it is a sermon in itself._

_When you see anyone who hates without reason, without even knowing the object of their hatred—reject that narrowness and that arrogance and that indecency. Throw it out and let the light of tolerance shine in our country and our souls._

*Think for a moment about these three words:*
*"No, thank you." That one sentence might save your life,*
*and it will definitely save your soul. Depending on punctuation*
*these words can be said different ways. Among the most*
*important is simply "No, thank you." When you encounter*
*meanness, cheating, when you are presented an opportunity*
*to do the wrong thing and get away with it, simply saying*
*"No, thank you" to yourself or the one tempting you to*
*behave badly will ensure you remain a mensch.*

---

*Trouble is neutral. It can do almost anything to us.*
*It can make us bitter and resentful. It can make us hard and*
*cruel. It can plunge us into despair and futility or it can*
*ennoble us and enable us to examine our lives and seek*
*a peace that has been so elusive for so long.*

---

*We call this creating* via negationis—*by the negative.*
*In other words, when we stop certain behaviors or remove*
*certain things and even certain people from our lives,*
*very often something else quite unexpectedly*
*beautiful emerges in their place.*

*Oh, I know—I know not everything that is broken can be fixed. I know that some families have been so dysfunctional for so long that nothing can save them. Some friendships can never be rescued; some betrayals cannot be overcome; some social problems are so deeply embedded they can never be uprooted. But I have also seen so many repair so much.*

---

*I looked out the window to see the waning moon,*
*reminding me that a new year will soon be upon us.*
*Between now and then, the moon will shift from waning to*
*waxing, from loss to gain. May that slim crescent of light, that*
*glimmer of hope against a black sky, remind us all to see what*
*is beautiful and good even in, especially in, the darkness.*

---

# CHAPTER 9

# How Do You Want to Be Remembered?

In my experience, a lot of people say that certain things, roles, and people are important to them, but if you examine how they spend their time, their emotional and their physical resources, it sure doesn't seem like it. The woman who says being a mother means more to her than anything in the world but spends far more time at the office or with friends than she does with her children. The man who claims to work hard in order to provide for his family but in truth already has enough money and works more for the power and ego gratification. There is the person who often says, "Family first," but hasn't called their parents or siblings in weeks or months. People who say they care passionately about creating a better world for the disadvantaged but their charitable giving is little to none. It's not so much that people are lying when they say they care about family or the disadvantaged, it's that when it comes to what we say is important and how we actually live, we are all out of alignment sometimes. Writing to your loved ones about how you want to be remembered is not only an opportunity for them to know and understand how you, in your finest moments, sought to live, but also for you to have more of those moments, to be aligned with your best self now, and for your loved ones later too.

When your loved ones want to envision you after you die, what do you want them to see? Where are you? How old are you? Whom are you with? What are you wearing? What are you doing?

_____

_____

_____

_____

_____

_____

_____

_____

_____

_____

_____

*In order to bring my father back to life, I merely have to remember all those simple things that he loved: a slice from a perfect avocado. A sunny day. Hank Williams and Johnny Cash. A joke—the dirtier, the better. Watching* All in the Family *in his vibrating Naugahyde chair, peeling an orange into a perfect spiral before handing out slices to each one of his five children as if we were a nest of hungry birds.*

*We live in a world that tries to convince us that time heals all wounds—it doesn't. A world full of "Don't be sad that it ended. Be glad it happened." We are sad. A world that says, "Feel better." We don't. A world that says, "At least she isn't suffering," while we wonder why she had to suffer at all and why we must suffer every day without her. We live in a world that mostly does not understand, that does not care, and that does not remember. Only we who miss them really understand. And right now, as the old year fades, day turning to dusk, sun settling into the earth, thousands of years of wisdom say, "Remember." What else can we do?*

---

*As a child, I rode shotgun with my father as we drove around Minneapolis on our way to fix things. Of course, first there were pancakes in the morning at the Town Talk Diner before we attacked the leaky faucet, the stuck door, or the clogged drain. And of course, there was mostaccioli and meatballs at Café di Napoli afterward for lunch. I was his scrub nurse: "Hand me those pliers. Give me that hammer. Hold the measuring tape right there."*

---

*For now, how else can we hold on to the people we love, to the past that defines us, the offenses that wound us, or the laughter and the love that warm us? How else can we hold on to anything in a world whose centrifuge of speed and stress tries to whirl us all apart? What else can I do when I miss my dad so much? What can any of us do who grieve today? Nothing, other than embrace this blessing, this curse, this imperfect gift, this burden, this holy vessel—memory.*

You know what else I loved about you when I was growing up, Mom? You always believed me, even when I was lying. You believed I would somehow turn out right. Your faith in me demanded my own self-respect. Your trust made me want to do the right thing even when I wasn't. How does a son thank his mother for believing in him?

_____

_____

_____

_____

_____

_____

_____

_____

_____

_____

_____

_____

_____

_____

_____

Joseph had a choice—essentially, he had a choice of memory. He had to choose whose wrong to remember: his arrogance or his brothers' jealousy. The wrong he inflicted or the wrong he suffered. He had to choose whether to remember the good or the bad, the sorrow or the joy, and then narrow it all down to one simple question: "Do I hold a grudge or do I forgive?"

---

*The world, our friends, the self-help books, our associates,
they all want us to move on, to move out of the house
of memories that is the only thing we have left to warm and
protect us. The world leaves us so little permission,
so little space, so little time, just—to remember.*

---

*Remember them before the disease, the dementia,
the accident, the CT scans, the doctors, the needles,
and the tubes. Remember them smiling, playing, advising,
in their favorite sweater, in their favorite chair, at their
favorite restaurant. Remember them laughing—just
laughing, hard and real with that sparkle in their eyes.*

# CHAPTER 10

# What Is Good Advice?

There is an old joke about a journalist who submits a story to her editor with an apology for its length. "Sorry," she explains. "I didn't have time to make it shorter." To be simple without being simplistic, to be concise, memorable, and truthful about the human condition is far more difficult than most people realize. Distilling your life lessons gained over decades of failure, victory, adversity, disappointment, and deep satisfaction is a challenge. It's no wonder we borrow other people's sayings when they have captured some complicated aspect of life in a perfect, short, and simple way.

My father was street-smart but barely finished high school. I, on the other hand, studied at some of the finest academic institutions in the world, resulting in two postgraduate degrees. And yet, despite our difference in formal education, my father and I both speak and teach mostly with hard-won advice in the form of an aphorism, a joke, or a folktale. The Bible is mostly written in short, stubby sentences with few multisyllabic words. It was meant to be heard more so than read. Share some simple advice with your loved ones so that they hear your voice and are guided by your heart now and always.

What are your top five sayings that encapsulate
the accrued wisdom of your life experience?

_____

_____

_____

_____

_____

_____

_____

_____

_____

_____

_____

_____

_____

_____

I am caught between two realities, both easy to prove yet diametrically opposed. Which is it? Which truth shall we build our lives upon—life is short, or life is long?

_____

_____

_____

_____

_____

_____

_____

_____

_____

_____

_____

_____

_____

_____

_____

---

*Why a blessing over something as ordinary as bread?*
*It's simple of course. . . . If we can be grateful for bread,*
*then we can be grateful for the other, greater blessings of*
*life as well. It is a wise person, a wise and a happier person,*
*a more successful person, a better person, who affirms*
*the enoughness, the beauty, the miracle of bread.*

---

*We are all, after all, only human.*

---

*What would the ancient prophets have to say to us today about our national bickering? They would remind us that the Second Temple in Jerusalem fell not because of Roman occupation but because of* sinat chinam—*infighting. They would remind us that the plague of darkness in the Passover tale was "A darkness so dark that people could not recognize the humanity in each other."*

---

*Reach down into the muck of our hurtful, broken family,*
*our broken city, our broken country, and our broken selves*
*where we hide so much, and promise that we will blister*
*our hands in the heat and the cold and fix something.*

---

*Real peace is a wholeness, an ethic, a marriage, a family, a workplace, a city, a country, a world that values and respects and honors different points of view and different human journeys. Do we pursue that kind of peace—the peace that comes from respecting and caring about the other?*

---

*Even when we do stop to count our blessings, we often count the wrong things. Two thousand years ago the Talmud reminded us that to be rich is to be satisfied with what we have already accomplished.*

---

*When you must, you can.*

---

A single deed the weight of a single feather can make all the difference. It is the same sort of thinking that led the rabbis of the Talmud to remind us that saving a single life is like saving the entire world. Or as my father would have put it in Yiddish, "A bissle iz a platz—*A little is a lot.*"

# CHAPTER 11

# What Will Your Epitaph Say?

Funerals are about the person who has died, but they are not for them. They are for the friends and family still alive to tell and to honor the story of the dead person's life. That is true for headstones too. We will never read what is carved upon the marker atop our grave. Its message is for the living.

Much like good advice, this too is an exercise in essentialism. When we must capture the essence of our life's purpose with just a few words, we leave behind a powerful message about what and who matters most. I see no reason to wait or to leave that task to others. Rather than make your loved ones guess, tell them now, with a few perfect words, whom and what you lived for. Let it be engraved in stone and upon their hearts.

What will your epitaph say? A headstone has room for
fifteen characters per line and four lines total.
What would you want it to say and why?

_____

_____

_____

_____

_____

_____

_____

_____

_____

_____

_____

_____

_____

_____

_____

_____

_____

_Each of us has our own unique way of living and loving and laughing and caring unlike anyone else who has ever lived or ever will live._

_You write your own eulogy with the pen of your life._

---

*When you have only fifteen characters per line to
sum up a person's life, you have to distill that life down
to its most essential elements. You want to know what
really matters? Walk through the cemetery and read the
headstones. It almost always comes down to a few
simple words. Loving husband, father, and grandfather.
Loving wife, mother, and grandmother. Loyal friend.
Loving sister. Loving brother. That's it.*

---

---

*I look in the mirror every morning—into my sometimes discouraged, sometimes optimistic, sometimes exhausted, sometimes joyful, flawed, foolish, arrogant, kind, loving, impatient eyes—and I see not only me, but my father too looking back at me. My face is now the face of my father that I recall from when I was a little boy and he is looking at me and he is asking me, have I behaved, have I achieved, have I been true to everything he taught me about being a man? It would be easier to turn away, but the mirror is me, it is my father, it is God and Torah all asking me who I really am.*

---

*The mystics believed someday each of us would grasp our spark, and then return that spark to all the others in a single brilliant light of everlasting wholeness and peace. We need that day now. We mean so much more together than we do apart.*

---

*Yes, sing your note from the tops of your lungs for all the world to hear. But for God's sake and our nation's too, be a part of the chorus, because together we sing a more glorious song.*

---

_Perfection has no place in this world. Despite the fact that perfection is a human creation, perfect creatures belong in heaven, not on Earth. This world is for those of us with imperfections. None of us is perfect, but we are all worthy._

---

*And so, this simple prayer: Help us, as we imagine our deaths, to make the most of our lives. Help us to remember the simplest of truths death comes to teach, so that what will be carved of us into stone will be written and sealed with love.*

---

CHAPTER 12

# What Will Your Final Blessing Be?

A blessing can be many things: a gift of talent or good fortune, a wish for Divine protection, or an OK from your boss. In its purest form, a blessing is an expression of gratitude unlike any other. Your ethical will is ultimately a blessing bestowed upon those you love, a wish for their protection, and a thank-you for all the meaning and the love, given and received. Bless them with your story. Bless them with your truth. Bless them with your legacy. Bless them for now, and bless them for when you are gone.

If you could speak to your family at the end of your own funeral, what would you say? What would your final blessing to them be?

_____

_____

_____

_____

_____

_____

_____

_____

_____

_____

_____

_____

_____

_____

_____

_____

_____

*Death is not the end but a different kind of living and loving, an invitation to remember, to see and to feel the depths of love that cannot die.*

*Those we love and have lost. They speak. They speak*
*to us through our own children, their grandchildren;*
*through dreams; through their kindness we sometimes did*
*not fully appreciate until relived and retold from the grave.*
*There is a life after death for those we love—a life lived*
*in our hearts and souls, dreams and daily life. And our*
*loved ones not only speak to us—they see. "They dwell,"*
*as the poet Tagore put it, "in the pupils of our eyes."*

*Choose blessings over curses, and life over death. It's not that evil doesn't exist. It's that good and we its ally can triumph over evil. Must we forgive what happened? We cannot forgive what is unforgivable. What we can do is choose this moment to count our blessings and ease the suffering of others.*

God asks only this of us—that we find some meaning in our suffering and our sins. That the pain we have inflicted and the pain we have endured cause us to examine our lives and make them beautiful, despite and because of our brokenness.

*"Dad, do you think the world is going to end?"*
*my twenty-one-year-old son asked me while sitting*
*at the kitchen table. "There are a lot of really bad things*
*happening." One of the most hopeful moments of my life*
*each year is something we call* **Kadimah**. **Kadimah** *is a Hebrew*
*word that means "forward—let's go forward." It's also the*
*name we use for our nursery school graduation ceremony.*
*Every year, all of the soon-to-be kindergartners line up in*
*front of their proud parents and grandparents and shout,*
**"Kadimah"** *as they take a giant step forward. For those young*
*children, shouting* **"Kadimah"** *with a giant step forward is a*
*sort of game. But for adults, for us, stepping into the future*
*is an act of faith. So no, my dear son, the world is not going*
*to end. For you, for me, for us, it is always* **Kadimah**—
*forward, forward with faith despite our fears.*

*Legend has it, in the time of King David, a hundred people died every day due to a terrible plague. So King David and the Sages instituted a spiritual "measure for measure" response: the saying of a hundred blessings each day. Suddenly, the plague stopped. To this day a traditional Jew says a hundred blessings a day. A blessing for awaking each day? Yes. For eating a strawberry? Yes. For the ways our bodies work? Yes. For narrowly avoiding a car crash? Yes. A tree swaying in the breeze? Yes.*

*My prayers are of gratitude for every moment of
every day until my last. I pray to cherish life.*

*The world around us, our friendships, our marriages, our brothers and sisters, our parents and children, are filled with shortcomings—with occasional pettiness and greed, frustration and anger. But so too are they filled with generosity and kindness, with caresses and comfort, self-sacrifice and love too constant, too deep, and too profound for words.*

*Let us use our hands and our lives to give, not to take,*
*and our hearts to find the holy and the good within us all.*

# A Final Note

Your answers to these questions as you've written them in this book can be your ethical will. Or you may choose to compile them in another format, perhaps edit them in some way. I wrote my ethical will in the form of a letter to my children; the questions are implicit but they're there, the same questions that have guided you here. I keep it on my computer and return to it from time to time to make revisions as I learn things and life changes me. I see it as a work in progress, but you might prefer "once and done." There is no wrong way to write your ethical will as long as you write the truth and speak from your heart.